Discovering and Serving Your Passion for Life:

A Catholic Stewardship Guide

By

Bradley L. Hahn

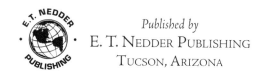

Published by
E. T. NEDDER PUBLISHING
TUCSON, ARIZONA

The Book Team
Ernie Nedder, Publisher
Kathy Nedder, CFO
Bradley L. Hahn, Author
Kate Harrison, Editor
Sharon Nicks, Designer

Copyright © 2005
E.T. Nedder Publishing
All rights reserved.

Originally published by Legacy Innovations, Inc., © Copyright 2004. No part of this book may be reprinted or transmitted in any form or by any means, electronic or mechanical, or by an information retrieval system without permission in writing from the publisher.

Additional copies of this publication may be purchased by sending check or money order for $9.95 to: Theological Book Service, P.O. Box 509, Barnhart, MO 63012. Or call toll free 1-888-247-3023. Fax: 1-800-325-9526. E-mail: bookstore@theobooks.org. Be sure to check our Web site for a list of other products: www.nedderpublishing.com.

Order #: 48-X
6 x 9
Individual copies: $9.95

ISBN: 1-893757-48-X

"A sensitive and thoughtful work committed to love, service, and stewardship; a provocative spiritual read." — *Robert A. Esperti, Esq.*

"Brad Hahn has done a masterful job of uniting the values of stewardship with core issues of estate planning. This book is a call to personal spiritual reflection as well as a tool for defining one's legacy as a faithful Catholic." — *John A. Scola CFRE, Executive Director, Catholic Community Foundation - Diocese of Phoenix*

"*Discovering and Serving Your Passion for Life: A Catholic Stewardship Guide* is inspirational and fulfilling. It defines the essence of stewardship by showing how Catholics can express their faith and beliefs in value-based estate planning. This book shows how a Catholic estate plan can combine a Faith Declaration with responsible lifetime and death planning. It is important reading for those Catholics who want to ensure that they can preserve and protect their faith, their talent, and their wealth for a greater purpose." — *Renno Peterson, Esq.*

PREFACE

Most estate plans do not capture the heart and soul of who we are. I searched to find ways to implement Catholic Christians' goals, dreams, aspirations, beliefs and faith into estate planning. Fortunately, after learning and teaching with many great people, I created this book for all Catholics to read and enjoy.

The goal of this book is to outline, with examples, how we can identify and use our time, talent and treasure to serve our world for the greater glory of our Lord. Many of the principles in this book are illustrated by my own faith journey as a Catholic. I have also included a number of exercises to help readers understand better the meaning of stewardship for Catholic Christians. By using these exercises, I have found greater meaning in my life and in my professional duties as an estate planning attorney while serving God's people.

Bradley L. Hahn, Esq.

ACKNOWLEDGMENTS

My special thanks to my wife, Julie, who always allows me to pursue my calling and my dreams. It is a great comfort knowing I experience God's love through her.

This book collects thoughts and concepts gleaned from many teachers and mentors I have met over the years, especially Scott Farnsworth, who showed me how to implement legacy planning into my estate planning practice, who is a friend and always available for personal and business advice. Also, I am grateful for the many teachers of the National Network of Estate Planning Attorneys, Inc. and Wealthcounsel, L.L.C., who allowed me to start a law practice right after law school and assisted me as my law practice grew.

Thank you also to Vickie Jennett from St. Timothy Catholic Community for assisting with the initial editing and design of this book.

TABLE OF CONTENTS

FOREWORD

Often when we talk about stewardship, we refer to its "Three Ts": time, talent and treasure. We are good stewards of our Catholic faith when we volunteer to teach a catechism course at our parish. We also display our stewardship when we share our accounting expertise by volunteering to serve on the parish finance council. And, we live our faith as good stewards every time we financially support the work of Christ.

In this book, Bradley Hahn shares with us the joy we can gain in sharing our treasure to more fully live our Christian faith. Brad, a Phoenix-area attorney and longtime national teacher on estate planning and stewardship, specifically outlines how to craft a Catholic Estate Plan that allows us to keep supporting the good works of our Church long after we pass from this world.

Think about it. We plan most every aspect of our lives, from the mundane – which route shall I take to work today? – to the life-changing – how will we raise our children? It's only logical that we would want to prayerfully discern how our treasure might make a difference in others' lives as well.

I recommend *Discovering and Serving Your Passion for Life: A Catholic Stewardship Guide* for anyone hoping to discover the sheer joy that comes in sharing your gifts with others.

Martin Camacho
Executive Director, Catholic Foundation for the Diocese of Tucson

INTRODUCTION

We usually refer to the Passion as the period between the last supper and the crucifixion of Jesus. However, passion can also describe a strong feeling, often love or even an object of affection or enthusiasm. As a Catholic, Christ's death is an act of love and can be an object of affection and enthusiasm for us because it was an incredible gift. He died for us and our sins. Dying for us displays passion for us. It takes passion for God to send his only son to our world to die for sinners. Consequently, God's passion for us can be returned to him through our bodies, thoughts and actions. If we follow Christ and his teachings, we can become passionate about him and the ultimate price he paid for our salvation. As disciples of Christ, we serve God and express our passion, faith and obedience to Him through stewardship. Stewardship is more than tithing. Our stewardship fulfills God's plan when we use our gifts and talents to serve Him. Discipleship is about defining and expressing our own stewardship in a manner that is pleasing to God.

It may be difficult to express our stewardship to the world if we do not know our calling or purpose for life. God has unique plans for each and every one of us. By discovering that plan, we can live a passionate life for God. The first step to discover your plan is to engage Jesus and ask him to be a part of your life. After we realize that Jesus must be a part of our daily activities, we must surrender our life to God and constantly pray for his guidance and grace as we encounter the world. By vigilant prayer and surrender, we can hope and pray that we will discover our unique stewardship and how God is asking us to serve him in our daily lives.

Stewardship takes on many forms in our lives. We are stewards when we teach our children our Catholic faith. We are stewards when we tithe. We are stewards when we serve food to the poor. We are stewards when we use our gifts and talents to make a living. We are also stewards when we complete our Catholic Estate Plan. Our stewardship is not finished when we pass away. Our estate planning must reflect our Catholic heritage in the money, property and values we leave.

This book allows Catholics to understand the basic principles of stewardship and shows how we use our time, talent and treasure to serve God. In the book, there are questions to uncover your gifts and talents and a discussion on how to implement those gifts and talents in your life. Reading this book and allowing time for prayer and personal reflection allows Catholics to connect to their stewardship calling while truly becoming disciples of Jesus Christ.

Discovering Your Passion

Discipleship and Stewardship

Having grown up in the Midwest, my fondest memories are of summers spent on my grandmother's farm. My grandfather died when I was 3, and Grandma had to run the family farm while providing for the family. My grandmother continues to work very hard on the farm, but she always has time to serve her church community. I remember seeing Grandma write a check to St. Boniface Church every week and watching how she helped at funerals when the person who passed away had little family remaining. I saw her bake delicious pies for funerals, weddings and other celebrations at the church. I particularly remember how her gooseberry pies raised hundreds of dollars at the church auction every Fourth of July. Even though my grandma is of modest means, I created an estate plan for her to ensure that her Catholic faith and stewardship will continue after she is gone. She is my role model, showing me how to be a good disciple and steward for our Lord.

Jesus calls us all to be His disciples, no matter what the cost. We must commit ourselves to the Lord with our minds and hearts, and become one with Him. We are called always to reflect on what it means to be His disciples. Stewardship is the way we answer our calling as disciples. Stewardship is an extension of our faith. The Bible reminds us "faith without works is dead." (James 2:26) Once we understand, appreciate and truly accept that all of our gifts are from God and they belong to Him, we can then give back to God by glorifying Him and showing our obedience and loyalty to Him. We are called to live as Christ's disciples, giving of our time, talent and treasure to become stewards of our vocation and of our Church. Scripture tells us that, "As each one has received a gift, use it to serve one another as good stewards of God's varied grace." (1 Peter 4:10)

Giving our gifts back to God may not always be easy, as Mother Teresa reminds us:

> That we may remain faithful to the gift of God, to love Him and serve Him in the poor together with you. What we have done we should not have been able to do if you did not share with your prayers, with your gifts, this continual abundance giving. But I don't want you to give me from your abundance, I want that you give me until it hurts. (Nobel Peace Prize Lecture, Dec. 11, 1979)

We must individually decide what "give until it hurts" means. For some, God may be calling us to sacrifice a few luxuries. For a select few, like St. Francis of Assisi, God may be calling us to give up our family fortunes and live a simple life of poverty and humility while serving the poor. We must determine through reflection and prayer the amount of time, talent and treasure we are able to give based on the circumstances in our lives. We must fully trust God and know in our hearts that He will provide for us. If we do sacrifice until it is uncomfortable, He will be there to ensure we receive blessings. We must truly understand that whatever we receive in our lives is a gift from God. We must freely give in order to receive His blessings and gifts.

> Consider this: whoever sows sparingly will also reap sparingly, and whoever sows bountifully will also reap bountifully. Each must do as already determined, without sadness or compulsion, for God loves a cheerful giver. Moreover, God is able to make every grace abundant for you, so that in all things, always having all you need, you may have an abundance for every good work. As it is written:

"He scatters abroad, he gives to the poor; | his righteousness endures forever."

The one who supplies seed to the sower and bread for food will supply and multiply your seed and increase the harvest of your righteousness.

You are being enriched in every way for all generosity, which through us produces thanksgiving to God, for the administration of this public service is not only supplying the needs of the holy ones but is also overflowing in many acts of thanksgiving to God. Through the evidence of this service, you are glorifying God for your obedient confession of the gospel of Christ and the generosity of your contribution to them and to all others, while in prayer on your behalf they long for you, because of the surpassing grace of God upon you. Thanks be to God for his indescribable gift! (2 Corinthians 9:6-15)

What is Stewardship?

God calls us to be stewards of both our vocation and of His Church. God calls us to be stewards of our vocation because he knows each one of us by name and we are responsible for carrying out His divine plan through our own personal vocation. "Before I formed you in the womb, I knew you." (Jeremiah 1:5) We must understand our role in His divine plan and respond graciously and generously with our time, talent and treasure.

God also calls us to be stewards of His Church. As members of His Church, we have roles as parents, parishioners and Catholics. As parents, we must impart God's teachings to our children. As parishioners, we must create parishes that imitate Christ's faith and service. As Catholics, we must serve the Universal Church. This is a difficult commitment because following Christ cannot be accomplished through isolated events in our lives; rather, it must become a way of life. In Medieval times, the stewards were responsible for the kingdom when the king was absent. Our King, Jesus Christ, no longer physically walks with us. Since our King is absent, it is our duty to run His kingdom. Are we giving our time, talent and treasure to His kingdom for His glory?

God asks us to convert our hearts to Him and to lose ourselves in giving His love to others. "Whoever seeks to preserve his life will lose it, but whoever loses it will save it." (Luke 17:33) This unconditional giving of His love shows respect to God and to others in our society. This is a very important task in furthering the kingdom of the Lord.

Not only must we follow stewardship while living, it is equally important to ensure that our stewardship is part of our legacy after we are gone. We have a responsibility to provide for our family: "And whoever does not provide for relatives and especially family members has denied the faith and is worse than an unbeliever." (1 Timothy 5:8) As Catholics, we have a responsibility to others to build a solid foundation for those who follow: "Tell them to do good, to be rich in good works, to be generous, ready to share, thus accumulating as treasure a good foundation for the future, so as to win the life that is true life." (1 Timothy 6:18-19)

Example of Stewardship

Take a look at how one woman's unselfish act of kindness illustrates being a disciple of Christ: A principal at a local Catholic high school decided to give her salary for three years to the school's foundation fund. There was very little money in the foundation fund when her contributions started. Certainly, sacrificing three years of her salary created some discomfort at the least or maybe even some hardship in her family's financial situation. Sacrifices likely were made because of this reduced income. Her donation, however, established a great foundation to help current and future students of the high school long after she leaves as principal. The principal gave her time, talent and treasure to serve God. While most of us cannot duplicate the principal's act, we must decide what we can do to serve the Lord in our own ways.

Our Time

An essential component of stewardship is using our time to serve our Lord. Where are we spending our free time? The U.S. Bishops' Pastoral Letter, *Stewardship: A Disciple's Response*, refers to a list of "ism's" that infiltrate our lives and take our time and energy from our stewardship. Materialism, relativism, hedonism, individualism and consumerism are prevalent in our society. These "ism's" were documented by Jim Spring, "Seven Days of Play," in *American Demographics* (March 1993) in a study showing how the average American spends his or her free time on a weekly basis:

- ♦ 12 hours watching television
- ♦ 6 hours socializing or eating out
- ♦ 5 hours shopping
- ♦ 4 hours watching movies or reading
- ♦ 3 hours on hobbies
- ♦ 2 hours on sports/exercise
- ♦ 1 hour on religious or volunteer activities

Our society pulls us in many directions and can leave us exhausted at the end of our day. While busy, are our days pleasing to God? We must examine our lives to determine where our time is spent and determine if there are hours in our week where we can fulfill our call to stewardship. Time must also be set aside to plan for our legacy to fulfill His divine plan after we pass away. God calls us to pass on our Catholic faith and beliefs to our loved ones so they may also follow Christ. God also expects us to plan how we can use our material wealth to further His divine plan.

The second part of stewardship is using our talents to please the Lord. What talents has God given you and how does He want you to use them to further His kingdom on earth? We must use our talents, and not bury them.

"It will be as when a man who was going on a journey called in his servants and entrusted his possessions to them. To one he gave five talents; to another, two; to a third, one—to each according to his ability. Then he went away. Immediately the one who received five talents went and traded with them, and made another five. Likewise, the one who received two made another two. But the man who received one went off and dug a hole in the ground and buried his master's money. After a long time the master of those servants came back and settled accounts with them. The one who had received five talents came forward bringing the additional five. He said, 'Master, you gave me five talents. See, I have made five more.' His master said to him, 'Well done, my good and faithful servant. Since you were faithful in small matters, I will give you great responsibilities. Come, share your master's joy.' [Then] the one who had received two talents also came forward and said, 'Master, you gave me two talents. See, I have made two more.' His master said to him, 'Well done, my good and faithful servant. Since you were faithful in small matters, I will give you great responsibilities. Come, share your master's joy.' Then the one who had received the one talent came forward and said, 'Master, I knew you were a demanding person, harvesting where you did not plant and gathering where you did not scatter; so out of fear I went off and buried your talent in the ground. Here it is back.' His master said to him in reply, 'You wicked, lazy servant! So you knew that I harvest where I did not plant and gather where I did not scatter? Should you not then have put my money in the bank so that I could have got it back with interest on my return? Now then! Take the talent from him and give it to the one with ten. For to everyone who has, more will be given and he will grow rich; but from the one who has not, even what he has will be taken away. And throw this useless servant into the darkness outside, where there will be wailing and grinding of teeth.' (Matthew 25:14-30)

Whatever talents God has given us, we must use them to further His kingdom in His glory. We must not ignore or neglect them. We all have talents that must be identified before we can glorify our God by using them to serve others. It is our responsibility to take time to reflect on our talents and implement those talents as service. When we fully embrace our God-given talents and use them for His glory, abundance will follow. When we wisely use Catholic Estate Planning to preserve and perpetuate the talents we have used to create something larger than ourselves, our talents can outlive us.

Example of Talent and Stewardship

A Catholic man attended the Bishop's Crozier Dinner and gave a sizable donation while in attendance. A representative from the Catholic Community Foundation followed up to thank the man as well as to learn more about him. This man had a passion for classical music and explained to the representative that when young children are exposed to classical music at an early age, their overall learning and retention increases. Catholic elementary schools were trying to implement a classical music program at that very moment, but lacked the proper financing. As you might expect, the man gave an additional donation to get the classical music program off the ground. Even when he passes away, his passion for classical music will continue and thrive in the lives of young Catholic students.

Our Treasure

The third part of Stewardship is tithing. Tithe means tenth. Tithing is a command from God. "Each year you shall tithe all the produce that grows in the field you have sown." (Deuteronomy 14:22) Tithing is biblically based and first appears in the Bible when Jacob vows, "If God remains with me, to protect me on this journey I am making and to give me enough bread to eat and clothing to wear, and I come back safe to my father's house, the LORD shall be my God. This stone that I have set up as a memorial stone shall be God's abode. Of everything you give me, I will faithfully return a tenth part to you." (Genesis 28:20-22)

Tithing is often considered an ugly word within the Church. Typically, we hear the word spoken when our parish priest —almost apologizing — gives the yearly financial tithing lecture. Many people still look negatively at giving up their resources and still have a "what's in it for me" attitude. Parishioners work hard for their money. Our fiscal responsibilities are pulled in many different directions and our resources are gone before we know it. Many questions are raised by the Catholic faithful. Why should we give it away? For what reason? Why should my pastor or church tell me how much and how often to give when it is my choosing?

As Catholic Christians, it is easy to talk the talk, but do we walk the walk when it comes to tithing? What we give hurts, even if we are not tithing a full 10 percent. We truly are trusting in the Lord when we give. We trust that the Lord has granted us our abundance and that in our giving, no matter how difficult, He will continue to provide for us. Always He shall provide for us so that we may provide for each other.

The following study by John and Sylvia Ronsvalle, *The Poor have Faces: Loving Your Neighbor in the 21st Century*, focused on how Americans spend their annual discretionary income:

♦ $44 billion on soft drinks
♦ $35 billion on sports activities
♦ $29 billion on diets
♦ $19.5 billion on lottery tickets
♦ $12 billion on candy
♦ $8 billion on pets
♦ $5.5 billion on video games
♦ $3.5 billion on cut flowers
♦ $2.7 billion on skin care
♦ $1.7 billion on missionary activities

Mother Teresa's Nobel Prize message contained this story:

The other day I received 15 dollars from a man who has been on his back for twenty years, and the only part that he can move is his right hand. And the only companion that he enjoys is smoking. And he said to me: "I do not smoke for one week, and I send you this money." It must have been a terrible sacrifice for him, but see how beautiful, how he shared, and with that money I bought bread and I gave to those who are hungry with a joy on both sides, he was giving and the poor were receiving. (Nobel Peace Prize Lecture, Dec. 11, 1979)

If a man can give up smoking for one week to feed the poor, can we give a portion of our lifestyle to serve others? These are difficult questions to address because our faith and existence are called into question. We are forced to look at ourselves with an objective eye and place our lives on the cross with Christ.

Our Stewardship Challenge

When determining what stewardship is in our lives, we must ask ourselves some very challenging questions:

✤ Am I truly a person of courage? A person of integrity?

✤ Am I truly a person of judgment? A person of dedication?

✤ As a people, as a society and as a Church, have we become so complacent as not to notice the ills of the world?

✤ Have we become so comfortable in our homes that we forget the homeless?

✤ Do we take our freedom for granted by forgetting those who are not free?

✤ Do we accept any decision by governments or religious bodies without questioning it as a moral act?

✤ Have we forgotten to use our voices, our time, our energy and our money to make this a better world?

After all, this is an example set for us by Jesus Christ. May we never lack the vision to see that things can and should be better. Every Catholic has this calling, to leave not just money behind but also a way of life, a living legacy. We must leave a tradition of involvement and responsibility — not just to our blood relations, but also to all humankind. Stewardship is about building a future, not just for you or me, but for those who come after. It is about setting the examples of "loving, learning, laboring, laughing, lamenting, linking, living and leaving." (*Legacy: The Giving of Life's Greatest Treasures* by Barrie Sanford Greiff, M.D.)

We easily become complacent in our tithing. Most Americans have never been without what we consider basic necessities: food, clothing and shelter. Other parts of the world are not as fortunate. We have become very comfortable in our lifestyles.

> When he [Jesus] looked up he saw some wealthy people putting their offerings into the treasury and he noticed a poor widow putting in two small coins. He said, "I tell you truly, this poor widow put in more than all the rest; for those others have all made offerings from their surplus wealth, but she, from her poverty, has offered her whole livelihood." (Luke 21:1-3)

Sharing our treasure with those who need assistance is one important resource we use in Catholic Estate Planning to perpetuate Christ's love through our actions. Christ emanates from within us when we serve others.

> Christ has no body on earth but yours;
> Yours are the only hands with which he can do his work,
> Yours are the only feet with which he could go about the world,
> Yours are the only eyes through which his compassion can shine forth upon a troubled world.
> Christ has no body on earth but yours.
> —Teresa of Avila (1515-1582)

Being Christ's body on earth to compassionately serve takes spiritual discipline. This is similar to a modern day warrior. A warrior, in the ancient sense must have integrity; meaning consistency in thought, word and action. (*In Search of the Warrior Spirit*, 203) It can seem overwhelming to be constantly risking and failing. (*Warrior Spirit,* 91) We can strive to be a living expression of our Christianity, to understand our mission for this world, to uncover our weakness and limitation along with our strengths. We must understand that it is OK to fail, because that gets us closer to uncovering what God wants us to become. A teacher once told me to be invulnerable, one must be fully vulnerable. In essence, when we break down our facades and try to be fully vulnerable, we are stronger. We can listen without judgment and be open to the teachings of others and the lessons God is trying to teach us daily. In fact, we are stronger because we are not expending tremendous amounts of energy defending ourselves. When we play sports, playing defensively seems to take more energy than creatively playing offense.

Passion – Engage Jesus

Some people just go through the motions in their lives without excitement or passion and as Thoreau explained, "…lead lives of quiet desperation." Many want an exciting life, but are waiting for someone or something to excite them. The bad news is someone or something will not excite them. Nor will they be sitting at home one day, bored, and someone will knock at the door and say, "Get off the couch, today you will start living because I have an exciting life planned for you!!"

The same is true for those who attend church. Only a small percentage of parishioners tithe the required 10 percent or are actively involved in ministry. Some churches in the eastern part of the United States are even closing. The problem is not religion, the media or our culture, the problem lies in individuals' passion for life. "Our soul longs for passion, for freedom, for life." (*Wild at Heart, Discovering the Secret of a Man's Soul*, 6) Our passion cannot come from us alone; it must come from God through our soul, our being. We need to march to His drumbeat, not ours. Serve Him and others, not ourselves. We need to release our passions. We need "…to offer your bodies as a living sacrifice, holy and pleasing to God, your spiritual worship. Do not conform yourselves to this age but be transformed by the renewal of your mind, that you may discern what is the will of God, what is good and pleasing and perfect." (Romans 12:1-2)

Sometimes events in our lives force us to realize that we are not satisfied with the person we have become; or we become frustrated with our status quo lifestyle of just getting by. The events can be the death of a loved one, a failed business or even public scandal. Experiencing this brokenness in our lives can inspire us to engage Jesus. Some call this hitting rock bottom, and we realize that we cannot rise from the rock bottom without help and guidance from God. Once we are willing to engage Jesus, we can be ready to face the demons in our own lives and have the faith and wisdom to move ahead. If we never feel this inner urge to change our situation, we will encounter the same results we have experienced throughout our lives. (*Warrior Spirit*, 19) Some define insanity as doing the same thing and expecting different results. We will keep on getting the same results unless we engage Jesus in our lives and ask him to guide and help us.

Our brokenness defines us. Everyone experiences brokenness in their lives, but how we respond to our brokenness is what defines us as Christians. Are we going to drown ourselves in self-pity or chemicals to numb our pain, or are we going to rise up from our unique circumstances and engage Jesus in our lives? Our circumstances don't define who we are; they reveal what we are made of. Until we engage Jesus out of our brokenness, "we will be self-centered, self-reliant and our strength will be our own." (*Wild at Heart*, 137) Christ is present in our brokenness and pain. He experienced the ultimate in brokenness at Calvary on the cross. Christ can heal all of our wounds if we let him.

The result of engaging Jesus can be exhilarating. We can find inner peace once we understand our stewardship calling because our serving and living our unique call to stewardship results in true joy and happiness because we are giving of ourselves to others. Fortunately, or unfortunately, that truth is usually only discovered when we experience brokenness in our lives and consciously choose to engage Jesus in to healing our brokenness. (*Life of the Beloved, Spiritual Living in a Secular World*, 109)

There are many obstacles to discovering our passion. We live in a very busy world. Some of us even find it hard to attend Mass every week. We are being pulled in every direction with work, play, family and church. We have an opportunity to prioritize our activities. Our most important activities should glorify God's name. God is calling us and always seeking us. God will always be there for us, even when we are not ready to experience His grace, because God, the all powerful, is ready for us without any prior notice needed. Even in all of our imperfections, we are still loved and sought by God. We are reminded of this in Luke:

> The tax collectors and sinners were all drawing near to listen to him, but the Pharisees and scribes began to complain saying, "This man welcomes sinners and eats with them." So to them he addressed this parable. "What man among you having a hundred sheep and losing one of them would not leave the ninety-nine in the desert and go after the lost one until he finds it? And when he does find it, he sets it on his shoulders with great joy and, upon his arrival home, he calls together his friends and neighbors and says to them, 'Rejoice with me because I have found my lost sheep.' I tell you in just the same way there will be more joy in heaven over one sinner who repents than over ninety-nine righteous people who have no need of repentance." (Luke 15:1-7)

God is seeking us. Everyone who is not serving God with their unique gifts and talents is like the lost sheep in the parable. God is waiting patiently for us to encounter his presence to serve His kingdom.

At a recent homily, my pastor asked if we are just "hanging out" with Jesus. By "hanging out," he used the example of teenagers hanging out at the local mall and asked if the teens at the mall really know each other or are simply just "hanging out." For example, are the teens discussing their personal situations and praying for each other? Or are they having superficial conversations with no meaning or substance? An indicator whether the teens are just hanging out is whether they will be in contact with their friends in 20 years. If the answer is no, then they are just hanging out. Teens could still be in contact with their friends if they engage each other both intellectually and spiritually. For example, do they know each others' pain, joy or excitement? What makes them unique?

The same is true for our relationship with Jesus. Are we just hanging out? Do we really know him? Does he know us? Are we just attending Mass and happen to be in the same building where others are expressing their spirituality? Are our thoughts hundreds of miles away during the homily? Scripture reminds us of the dangers of just hanging out with Jesus:

> He passed through towns and villages, teaching as he went and making his way to Jerusalem. Someone asked him, "Lord, will only a few people be saved?" He answered them, "Strive to enter through the narrow gate, for many, I tell you, will attempt to enter but will not be strong enough. After the master of the house has arisen and locked the door, then will you stand outside knocking and saying, 'Lord, open the door for us.' He will say to you in reply, 'I do not know where you are from.' And you will say, 'We ate and drank in your company and you taught in our streets.' Then he will say to you, 'I do not know where [you] are from. Depart from me, all you evildoers!'"(Luke 13:22-27)

Will Jesus know us when we knock on heaven's door? I pray so. To ensure he will know us, we need to engage Jesus and get to know him. We need to experience his grace and abundance for he will be patiently waiting for us to engage him. Each and every one of us has a calling, a vocation to fulfill. The key is how to discover it. Paul writes that: "We always pray for you, that our God may make you worthy of his calling and powerfully bring to fulfillment every good purpose and every effort of faith, that the name of our

Lord Jesus may be glorified in you, and you in him, in accord with the grace of our God and Lord Jesus Christ." (2 Thessalonians 1:11-12)

A vocation, or how we make a living serving God, can be our calling in life if we find out what truly excites us. For example, a neighbor of ours has three engineering degrees, but was not truly satisfied in that career. She called it a career because she did not have passion at work. After discernment and prayer, she realized that God was calling her to teach math to junior high students. By talking to her about her new vocation, it is hard not to see her enthusiasm for the students (and God).

It is amazing the number of people who want to be rich in wealth and status. While channel surfing one can almost always find an infomercial trying to sell us some technique or strategy for instant wealth. The infomercials tell us that this is a way to happiness in our society. The question I always have while watching these promotions is, "Does God want me to have instant riches, wealth or fame?" For some wealth can be a heavy burden or even a curse. Most of us have heard about the lottery winners' demise into bankruptcy, divorce and other problems.

The Bible tells us about the rich young man who observes the commandments but he is still concerned that he will not attain the heavenly kingdom.

> Jesus said to him, "If you wish to be perfect, go, sell what you have and give to [the] poor, and you will have treasure in heaven. Then come, follow me." When the young man heard this statement, he went away sad, for he had many possessions. Then Jesus said to his disciples, "Amen, I say to you, it will be hard for one who is rich to enter the kingdom of heaven. Again I say to you, it is easier for a camel to pass through the eye of a needle than for one who is rich to enter the kingdom of God." (Matthew 19:21-24)

Does this mean that the rich cannot enter the kingdom of

God? Of course not! One of Jesus' followers was rich: Joseph of Arimathea. (See Matthew 27:17)

The point is not whether we can be wealthy or not, it is whether we follow God's calling. A better question may be what we need to give up for the love of Christ. In other words, what in our life interferes with God? It not only could be money like the parable above, but it could also be friendships that slow your spiritual growth or a job that contributes to sin, business practices that do not comport to Catholic Christian values or addictions or even disobeying a Church teaching because you do not agree with it. (*Daily Reflections*, www.goodnews.net, Aug. 16, 2004, by Terry A. Modica)

"Much will be required of the person entrusted with much, and still more will be demanded of the person entrusted with more." (Luke 12:48) This verse not only can relate to wealth accumulation, but also to our gifts and talents. We are entrusted with gifts and talents from God. We should identify what those gifts and talents are and use them to serve. Only when we serve our God fully with our time, talent and treasure, will we experience His grace and abundance in this world.

Pray and Surrender

After the conscious decision to engage Jesus in our lives, we must incorporate a vibrant prayer life so we can get to know and understand God (and ourselves) better. The Bible reminds us to "pray without ceasing." (1 Thessalonians 5:17) There are three forms of prayer: vocal, meditation and contemplative. A well-rounded prayer life should incorporate all three forms.

Vocal prayer satisfies our human need to express our feelings and emotions externally and is the most common used in groups, i.e., the Mass. God gave us our five senses to experience Him: taste, smell, touch, sight and hearing. We use all of our senses when we experience God at Mass. We taste Him through the Holy Communion. We smell him through the incense and candles burning. We touch Him when we shake the hands of others at the Sign of the Peace. We see Him through Holy Communion and colors He created around the altar. We hear Him through the Word and vocal prayer. At Mass, we use vocal prayer because it is the most common when a group of people gather. An example of vocal prayer is the "Our Father" that we regularly recite.

Another form of prayer is meditation prayer. Meditation engages our thought, imagination, emotions and desire. (*Catechism of the Catholic Church*, 2708) Meditation prayer helps us figure out why we lead a Christian life and how God is asking us to respond in our lives to His teachings. Some examples of meditation prayer are: Bible verses, rosary, books written by our saints, and holy icons. The Bible can be meditation prayer because the messages and teachings can assist us when we take our Christian faith to the world. For example, the Gospel reading in Matthew 23:27-32 discusses hypocrisy as being a "whitewashed tomb" which can signify a holy appearance on the outside but be deadly on the inside.

I apply this reading in my own life because I have a tendency to fall into hypocrisy when defending our Catholic faith. I can be defensive and unrelenting while discussing the tenants of our beliefs. This can be hypocrisy because instead of fully listening to others about their concerns and thoughts like Christ would listen, I am defensive which may possibly prevent me from being hurt. We must be fully vulnerable to others, even when we believe we are right and they are wrong. We must fully give ourselves to others with unconditional love and kindness so we can experience God's love in others. Remember, Jesus is always there for us to heal our wounds when others hurt us. (*Daily Reflections*, www.goodnews.net, Aug. 24, 2004, by Terry A. Modica) I receive an e-mail daily from www.goodnews.net which lists the scripture readings from the daily Catholic Mass. Along with the readings from the United States Conference of Catholic Bishops, Terry A. Modica offers a reflection relating to the readings.

> Meditation prayer can help us discover more about ourselves. We must be aware that following Christ does not mean we have any holes in our faith or spirituality, it means that we are aware of our holes.
>
> (*Warrior Spirit*, 175)

The final form of pray is contemplative prayer. This can be the most difficult form of prayer. We need prayer to sustain our relationship with God. It is the time we spend with Him like the time we spend cultivating our relationship with our family around the dinner table. St. Teresa believes prayer is a "close sharing between friends." (*St. Teresa of Jesus, The Book of Her Life*, 8, 5, in the *Collected Works of St. Teresa of Avila*) I look at contemplative prayer as a moment when we just simply take a break from our daily trials and ask the Holy Spirit to enter our hearts to release all of our fears, dreams and hopes into the hands of God. In order to experience God, we must empty ourselves (our heart) from all distractions and let his grace fill it back up. This form of prayer allows us to listen to God and to develop a friendship with Him and can also be the most difficult because it is hard to sit silently if our minds our constantly wandering and focusing on our daily trials.

One of my favorite examples of prayer is Mary's prayer at the wedding at Cana: "They have no wine." (John 2:3). Notice that Mary did not put condition on the prayer. She didn't say, "Jesus, we need wine right now," or "We need the best wine in the country." Rather, she just simply stated her prayer. God, all- knowing and all-loving, knows our troubles and concerns and what we need in this world. We do not have to pray for specific conclusions because our creator knows how to answer our prayers better than we do. (cf. Matthew 6:8) So, it may help if we pray for passion and excitement in our lives.

The first step in creating passion in your life and being a body that is a perfect living sacrifice to God is to pray. "But I will call upon God, | and the LORD will save me. | At dusk, dawn, and noon | I will grieve and complain, | and my prayer will be heard." (Psalms 55:17-18)

We must abandon ourselves to God and trust everything in Him. A good prayer to seek your calling from God is the prayer of abandonment by Brother Charles of Jesus (Charles de Foucauld):

Abandonment Prayer
Father, I abandon myself into Your hands;
do with me what You will.
Whatever You do I thank You.
I am ready for all, I accept all.
Let only Your will be done in me,

as in all Your creatures,
I ask no more than this, my Lord.
Into Your hands I commend my soul;
I offer it to You, O Lord,
with all the love of my heart,
for I love You, my God, and so need to give myself—
to surrender myself into Your hands,
without reserve and with total confidence,
for You are my Father.

This prayer may help us find His will and not ours if we tune in to what God is asking us to do. Another prayer that may help is the Prayer of Jabez. This prayer comes with a warning that your world will change if you truly believe in this prayer.

Prayer of Jabez
O that You would bless me indeed,
and enlarge my territory,
that Your hand would be with me,
and that You would keep me from evil,
that I may not cause pain!

This prayer had a profound effect on me. Within one week of incorporating the Prayer of Jabez into my prayer life my law partner changed the locks on the office and severed our partnership. I questioned God, whether He was blessing me and enlarging my territory. It was difficult to see at the time, but that was one of the best things that ever happened in my life because in the brokenness, I experienced Jesus. After that event, I kept praying the Prayer of Jabez and more abundance and blessing poured into my life than I could possibly imagine. I was impressed that when you ask God for help, He has a way of tearing down unhealthy situations for you even if you cannot see them at the time.

How we respond to devastation and tragedy in our lives can

be our true measure of success. Instead of sulking in the tragedy and feeling discontent with our lives, we can respond gloriously to the teachings of God, for He knows best. (*Wild at Heart*, 106). When presented with unfortunate events, I encourage you to pray for some guidance when you ask these questions to God:

1. What are you trying to teach me here?

2. What issues in my heart are you trying to raise through this?

3. What is it you want me to see?

4. What are you asking me to let go of?

5. How have I mishandled my wounds from the past? (*Wild at Heart*, 105-106)

Surrender is a condition of discipleship because we are fully in tune with what God's will is, and we are serving God's will for us. Surrender is necessary for a vibrant spiritual life as Jesus reminds us. "Then he said to all, 'If anyone wishes to come after me, he must deny himself and take up his cross daily and follow me. For whoever wishes to save his life will lose it, but whoever loses his life for my sake will save it.'" (Luke 9:23-24)

Abandoning ourselves and surrendering to God's will can be difficult. We cannot simply surrender to God and then forget about it. It is not a one time discussion with God and you are done. By surrendering, you wake up and give the day to God to follow His will, not yours.

Purpose

Don't ask yourself what the world needs. Ask yourself what makes you come alive, and go do that, because what the world needs is people who have come alive. (*Wild at Heart*, 200) The people that seem to have the most passion for life also seem to be following what God wanted them to do. Talents and gifts are given by God to be shared with everyone.

> You are the light of the world. A city set on a mountain cannot be hidden. Nor do they light a lamp and then put it under a bushel basket; it is set on a lampstand, where it gives light to all in the house. Just so, your light must shine before others, that they may see your good deeds and glorify your heavenly Father. (Matthew 5:14-16)

Our gifts and talents are God's light emanating from our soul shining out of ourselves for His glory. We should be His shining light. St. Francis of Assisi once said, "Preach the gospel, and use words if you have to." The best example we can be is to have our gifts and talents serve our church and the world. Conversely, the harshest criticism we find in the scripture is the man who buried his talents, "You wicked, lazy servant!" (Matthew 25:26)

> What is our unique talent? However, when focusing on talents, we tend to forget that our real gift is not so much what we can do, but who we are. The real question is not "What can we offer each other? But "Who can we be for each other?" ... We may have only a few talents, but we have many gifts. Our gifts are the many ways in which we express our humanity. They are part of who we are: friendship, kindness, patience, joy, peace, forgiveness, gentleness, love, hope, trust, and many others. These are the true gifts we have to offer each other. (*Life of the Beloved*, 113)

We can strive to be a Community of Disciples and have our lives filled with love while we share our faith, understanding and gifts with others. Our giftedness assists others in their time of need. The Good Samaritan story in Luke is a great example of sharing our love with others.

> "... A man fell victim to robbers as he went down from Jerusalem to Jericho. They stripped and beat him and went off leaving him half-dead. A priest happened to be going down that road, but when he saw him, he passed by on the opposite side. Likewise a Levite came to the place, and when he saw him, he passed by on the opposite side. But a Samaritan traveler who came upon him was moved with compassion at the sight. He approached the victim, poured oil and wine over his wounds and bandaged them. Then he lifted him up on his own animal, took him to an inn and cared for him. The next day he took out two silver coins and gave them to the innkeeper with the instruction, 'Take care of him. If you spend more than what I have given you, I shall repay you on my way back.' Which of these three, in your opinion, was neighbor to the robbers' victim?" He answered, "The one what treated him with mercy." Jesus said to him, "Go and do likewise." (Luke 10:30-37)

We all feel the need to be touched by a compassionate God. Not only do we need to help others feel our compassionate God, Jesus orders us to help others. Experiencing God does not only occur in church through ministry, but ministry needs to be taken from the church to the people of the world in our daily lives. This is what the Good Samaritan did. This is how we share the gospel message. God's grace and compassion is everywhere in our lives, we just need to be more aware of His presence. We can realize that God is part of our life when we ask ourselves these questions:

Where have I experienced Jesus?

Where have I experienced his compassion?

Where have I shown compassion to others?

Uncover Our Gifts and Talents

Before you can implement your stewardship in your life, you must first identify what your gifts and talents are. The following questions may assist you.

✤ What have you been hesitating to undertake in your life that you truly care about?

✤ If you were to die tomorrow, what would you regret not having done?

✤ What do you see as your deepest purpose in the coming years?

✤ What is unfinished for you to give? To learn? To experience?

✤ What people do you want to surround yourself with who could bring the most out of you?

✤ What do you value the most?

✤ What situations or environments bring out the best in you?

✤ What do you love that you want to make more alive and real?

✤ What would have to happen in your life in the coming years for it to become more meaningful?

✤ What gifts and talents are yearning to be expressed?

(Special thanks to Dawna Markova, *I Will Not Die an Unlived Life*, for inspiration for these questions.)

Uncovering our God-given gifts and talents is a great foundation for following the plan God has for us. However, putting those talents and gifts into action can sometimes be difficult. We may not know what God wants us to do. We may prejudge ourselves into thinking we cannot attain some lofty goal. We may be afraid to grow and reach our true potential. Whatever reasons we have for not using our gifts and talents, scripture tells us to forge ahead with our plans for the future, to pray, and to ask God to fulfill our plans.

"Ask and it will be given to you; seek and you will find; knock and the door will be opened to you. For everyone who asks, receives; and the one who seeks, finds; and to the one who knocks, the door will be opened." (Matthew 7:7-8)

Once we have the courage to dream about our plans for the future, we then must take the next steps to achieve our greatness. We must determine where we are in our lives in areas that are important to us like family, friends, spirituality, stewardship and even hobbies. Our next step is to determine where we want to be in these areas in the future. We have to be careful not to set limitations or assumptions on our dreaming. After we determine our future goals, write out the steps and deadlines it will take to accomplish them.

Scripture reminds us to plan our future so that we can fulfill the plan God has for us. "The plans of the diligent are sure of profit, | but all rash haste leads certainly to poverty." (Proverbs 21:5) Planning your future does not have to be a lonely process. Seek others to challenge your limiting assumptions. "Plans fail when there is no counsel, | but they succeed when counselors are many." (Proverbs 15:22)

Catholic Legacy Declaration™

"[Jesus] knows people's personal histories, their strengths and weaknesses, their destinies; he has a purpose in mind for each one." (*Stewardship: A Disciple's Response*, 13) Jesus knows our purpose. But, do we know? Determining our vocation and our talents can be a challenge. To find our calling, we must look back through our lives and think about our life story. Prayer is an essential part of the process. We pray to understand our calling as Christian disciples and for a conversion of our hearts to answer God's call. The following Stewardship Prayer may help us search for our own purpose in life:

Stewardship Prayer

Oh Lord, giver of life and source of our freedom,
we are reminded by the Psalmist that Yours is
"the earth and its fullness;
the world and those who dwell in it."
We know that it is from Your hand that we
have received all we have and are and will be.
Gracious and loving God, we understand that
You call us to be stewards of Your abundance,
the caretakers of all You have entrusted to us.
Help us always to use Your gifts wisely
and teach us to share them generously.
May our faithful stewardship bear witness to
the love of Christ in our lives.
We pray with grateful hearts, in Jesus' name. Amen.
(*The Disciple as Steward*, Sharon Hueckel)

I discovered my stewardship calling in life when I worked on my Catholic Legacy Declaration™. A Catholic Legacy Declaration™ is the process of reflecting on and praying about your calling and then articulating your story into written form. I did not set out intending to write a Catholic Legacy Declaration™. I went through training on how to implement clients' life stories into my legal estate planning practice. Preparing for the program, I completed a questionnaire. A few weeks after the program, I received the first draft of my Legacy Declaration. Answering the questions was a routine experience, but when I received the four-page typewritten document, something changed inside of me. I realized that I had so much to be thankful for and that God had truly blessed my life with both gifts and talents. Sadly, though, reading the document made me realize I was not giving my talents back to God as much as I could.

While we often dismiss our accomplishments in our minds, once they are written down, our achievements emerge with new meaning. For me, this meaning became increasingly clear the more I read my declaration. I was deeply touched when thinking about what God had allowed me to accomplish in the past and what possibilities the future might hold for me. I discovered that my heritage meant a lot to me because it taught me so much. My Catholic faith took on a new meaning in my life, and I wanted to help others write and preserve their stories while encouraging planned giving and development for the Catholic Church. My story told me that I enjoy communicating with people, and I especially enjoy teaching. I also love helping others fulfill their goals. I determined that my vocation is to share with others how estate planning can help families achieve their goals of providing for their families, while at the same time helping charities that are dear to their hearts. I really enjoy helping others identify their talents and treasures, and align them with their material wealth. I have found a deeper meaning and understanding about my life. This is my vocation, my calling to serve Christ.

Because many of us are geographically spread out across the nation and do not live near our relatives, taking time to share our life experiences is one of the best gifts we can give one another. In answering the call of stewardship, it is our responsibility to leave our faith to our loved ones. "And whoever does not provide for relatives and especially family members has denied the faith and is worse than an unbeliever." (1 Timothy 5:8)

Catholic Legacy Declaration Questions

The following are some questions to help you when you write your own Catholic Legacy Declaration™:

What does being a Catholic mean to you?

How important is it to you to see that your loved ones follow the teachings of the Catholic Church?

What is an important lesson you learned early in life?

How does it continue to influence your beliefs and values? Who taught you this lesson?

Who were two or three influential people in your childhood? How were they influential?

Looking back, which of your accomplishments do you find the most gratifying?

Looking ahead, name something you would like to accomplish or see happen during the rest of your life.

Describe your proudest moment.

What are a few of the most important ideas or lessons you would like to pass on to your children, grandchildren, or other loved ones?

What are some organizations, causes, issues or activities that you have found especially meaningful?

What concerns do you have about the distribution of your material wealth as part of your legacy?

You do not have to answer every single question and you may want to insert questions unique to your experience. As an example, here is an excerpt from my Catholic Legacy Declaration™.

THE CATHOLIC LEGACY DECLARATION™
OF BRADLEY L. HAHN

Purpose

I, BRADLEY L. HAHN, wish to leave to my family, friends and associates, a declaration of the principles and values that have guided my life. It is my hope and prayer that these few words will serve as a beacon to illuminate the way for others who may follow me on life's path and as a bridge to lift them over any bogs and chasms that may encumber their journey.

Prayer

Prayer has helped me out in my difficult times. I have always prayed the rosary, but in difficult times it gives me comfort knowing that I am giving my problems to God. It also comforts me when I use the rosary that my great-grandmother made for my First Communion. She made it out of purple beads because that was my favorite color. My great-grandmother Schomer made more than 100,000 rosaries in her lifetime. She is now gone, but the tradition of rosary making is now being passed on to my grandmother and my mother. It is powerful to think my family has helped so many others pray. I am especially mindful of the rosaries I have from my great-great-grandparents. They used these rosaries when they lived in Germany, and I feel a connection to them when I use them.

What I Learned

From my parents I have learned to work hard, play hard and have fun. My grandparents taught me to work hard to make a living for a family and to make life easier for my children. I am definitely the product of my heritage. I was raised to be strong in my Catholic faith, and today I am very active in the ministries of my parish, St. Timothy Catholic Community.

My Treasure

These and many other experiences have taught me the importance of values. I believe spiritual values such as faith, belief in God and inner peace to be of the greatest importance. I also consider ethical values such as honesty, fairness and justice to be of great significance. In addition, I believe that philanthropic values such as volunteer work and donations of my time, talent and treasure are also of greatest importance. I consider myself fortunate to have had several meaningful associations within my community. I have served meals to the poor at Paz de Cristo; I am a Eucharistic

Minister captain and marriage preparation minister for couples in my faith community. Finally, I have enjoyed working with the Catholic Community Foundation for the Diocese of Phoenix.

To My Children

If I am able to leave material gifts to my heirs, I hope these resources would aid them in their comfort of life. On the other hand, I am concerned that a financial legacy might spoil them or cause them to rely on the legacy alone. I believe that not assisting them in dealing with wealth would be a foolish approach in arranging to leave material gifts behind for my loved ones. The wiser course would be to allow the wealth to give my heirs the flexibility to be good stewards with the money.

I encourage you to pray for a conversion of your heart to understand your call to stewardship. As part of your current stewardship efforts, set aside time to reflect about your vocation as a Catholic and your service to your parish, your family and your world. After you reflect on the questions, I encourage you to write your own story. Stories have a powerful impact on our thinking. We can relate better to stories than to fragmented thoughts or legal documents. Writing your story with a blank piece of paper in front of you can be a daunting task. You may wish to consult estate planners (attorneys, accountants and financial advisors) to assist you when you write your Catholic Legacy Declaration™.

By completing this exercise, you can prepare the first draft of your Catholic Legacy Declaration™. Because this is a "living document," you may want to revise or amend it. Although this Declaration will secure a place in the minds and hearts of your family and close friends later on, you may also choose to share it with them now, as it can have a profound effect on how they see you.

Results of Your Catholic Legacy Declaration™

Your Catholic Legacy Declaration™ will help you to:

✣ uncover your talents so you can implement them to serve God as His steward;

✣ experience a conversion in your heart as you review your life and find more ways to serve as a steward;

✣ gain a clearer understanding of your own vision and values;

✣ build a bridge, reconnect or deepen your bonds with family members and friends;

✣ close some of the distance created by geographic separation of family and friends;

✣ enjoy the peace of mind that comes through knowing your loved ones will be aware of your beliefs;

✣ remember who you are, including the things that matter to you most.

What's next? After you think and pray about your vocation to fulfill God's divine plan, it is time to act. God is calling us to serve our family, our Church and our world. Identify where you can immediately help others. Ask others how you can help.

If you choose, this is the time to find an estate planning professional who focuses on Catholic issues. This person should be one who is willing to help you formulate, clarify and document all aspects of your Catholic Legacy to include aligning your wealth with your stewardship.

Properly prepared and documented, the Catholic Estate Plan is a great opportunity to teach loved ones about Christ and Catholic beliefs. Write down how much your Catholic faith means to you, and discuss how it has helped get you through difficult times in your life. Explain how that faith brings you satisfaction and joy. Show your loved ones that you are a disciple of Christ.

Serving Your Passion

Estate Planning Stewardship

Death is not the final chapter of our life. After death we realize God's truths and become fully alive in the Holy Spirit. We will also realize what gifts and talents the Lord gave us and will understand how and why we used them, or did not use them.

There was a rich man who dressed in purple garments and fine linen and dined sumptuously each day. And lying at his door was a poor man named Lazarus, covered with sores, who would gladly have eaten his fill of the scraps that fell from the rich man's table. Dogs even used to come and lick his sores. When the poor man died, he was carried away by angels to the bosom of Abraham. The rich man also died and was buried, and from the netherworld, where he was in torment he raised his eyes and saw Abraham far off and Lazarus at his side. And he cried out, "Father Abraham, have pity on me. Send Lazarus to dip the tip of his finger in water and cool my tongue for I am suffering torment in these flames." Abraham replied, "My child, remember that you received what was good during your lifetime while Lazarus likewise received what was bad; but now he is comforted here, whereas you are tormented. Moreover, between us and you a great chasm is established to prevent anyone from crossing who might wish to go from our side to yours or from your side to ours." He said, "Then I beg you, father, send him to my father's house, for I have five brothers, so that he may warn them lest they too come to this place of torment." But Abraham replied, "They have Moses and the prophets. Let them listen to them." He said, "Oh no, father Abraham, but if someone from the dead goes to them, they will repent." Then Abraham said, "If they will not listen to Moses and the prophets, neither will they be persuaded if someone should rise from the dead." (Luke 16:19-31)

Even the dogs gave Lazarus something — love — while the rich man stepped over him daily. What gifts are we asked to share? It may not be our wealth, because that may not be a gift that God has given us. Our gift could be the wisdom to help the poor like Lazarus. The most important message about the parable is we will be accountable for our use of our gifts when we meet our maker.

As Catholic Christians, we believe that Jesus Christ conquers death. He is the final YES while we approach the Kingdom of God in heaven. It is very difficult for many in our society to talk about death. We rarely take enough time to mourn when we lose a family member or friend. We are encouraged to continue as if nothing happened. (*Life of the Beloved*, 116) God's love for us is stronger than our death. The disciples understood this. We need to fulfill the plan God has for us and ensure our gifts and our love continue after our death because we can leave a legacy of our life to the ones we love and even our church.

In order for us to fulfill our role as stewards of our vocation and of our Church, we could complete a Catholic Estate Plan. Our role as stewards is no different whether we are alive or dead because our legacy still affects others. We must use our gifts from God wisely to help others now and after our death. We must take care of God's Church and fulfill our roles as parents, parishioners and Catholics.

Our role as parents is important because God tells us, "The good man leaves an inheritance to his children's children." (Proverbs 13:22) Inheritance is broader than our property and money, even though this is what we often think about when discussing estate planning. Inheritance includes not only our material wealth, but also our heritage, community and family. We are called to lovingly impart our faith to our children and our children's children. "...Do not provoke your children to anger, but bring them up with the training and instruction of the Lord." (Ephesians 6:4)

Catholic Faith Declaration™

The Unthinkable

Not long ago, my wife, Julie, delivered a healthy baby boy, Andrew James. We were both exhausted and I went home to take a nap and a shower. When I returned to the hospital just hours later, I found six nurses surrounding my wife and another mopping blood off the floor. Julie was hemorrhaging. From the looks on the nurses' faces, I knew it was far more serious than they would admit. The doctor arrived and they rushed my wife to emergency surgery to try to save her life. I thought, "These things only happened in old western movies, not today with modern technology and especially with a strong, healthy and young woman like Julie."

My wife, in tears, looked at me and closed her eyes thinking that this may be the last time we would see each other and she prayed, "Jesus, I am not ready to leave my family, but if it is my time, I am ready." Julie then felt a wave of peace through her body from head to toe and she prayed, "Mary, Mother of God, watch over me and my family." A soft and gentle voice she never heard before comforted her and told her everything would be all right. Through a miracle, her life was spared.

Not Prepared

I used to think we were prepared for death since I am an estate planning attorney, but how wrong I was. Before the baby came, Julie and I had all of our legal estate planning documents in order. What she had not done, however, was to create a Catholic Estate Plan. For example, my wife had not written how she wanted her Catholic faith expressed in the event of a disability or death. I knew she adored the Holy Eucharist, but I did not know if she wanted Holy Communion if she were disabled. I thought of her funeral and wondered how to express her Catholic faith. I knew her favorite songs, but I did not know which ones to play at her funeral. Her memorial service would be the last physical connection between her and earth. I felt an enormous responsibility to pray and think about what her Catholic wishes would have been.

I was scared that we had missed our chance to discuss and write down her faith. I was scared that my wife would never teach and show our children her Catholic faith. She had nothing written on how important her Catholic faith was to her and I knew I could not share her faith with our children as well as she could. I thought about scripture, "And whoever does not provide for relatives and especially family members has denied the faith and is worse than an unbeliever." (1 Timothy 5:8) I wondered whether we were living up to our faith.

I believe that as Catholics, our estate planning should reflect our Catholic heritage in the money, property and values we leave. We can and should leave instructions on how we want our faith to be followed during a disability and after our death. As Catholics, we need to address issues unique to our faith. For example, we believe that bread and wine are transformed in the body and blood of Jesus Christ at every Mass. Since the Eucharist is so sacred to us as Catholics, what happens if we are unable to attend Mass because of a disability? Would you still want to receive communion? This and many other concerns about our faith must be addressed to reflect our deepest beliefs.

Miracle

The day my wife went into labor, a statue of the Virgin Mary arrived at our house. We had been on the waiting list for more than two years to have the statue in our home. The statue was hand-carried from Medjugorje and it was our week to display it in our home. My wife admires the Virgin Mary and we have talked at times that we should pray the Rosary together, but just never found the time. We really believe that the Virgin Mary wished for that statue to be with us during this difficult time for our family.

My wife lost more than 90 percent of her blood and it is truly a miracle that she is alive today. She was given a second chance. She has a renewed conviction for our faith and the strong desire to share our story with our loved ones. Since that frightening day when death seemed so close, Julie has written down her Catholic wishes and has started to write her Catholic story. Her faith will be followed if we are not around to make those decisions. Our children will have their mother's teachings to follow, even if she is not here to speak them.

Opportunity for a Second Chance

I believe each of us, as committed Catholics, has a wonderful opportunity to create our own Catholic Estate Plan that reflects our Catholic beliefs. It is a legacy for the loved ones we leave behind. Unlike my wife, we do not often get a second chance.

All too often, family members must make very difficult decisions when a loved one becomes disabled or dies. When no thoughtful instructions are provided, family members may be left in a quandary: "I really don't know what she would want us to do now. I know she attended Mass every week, but we never asked her about it. I wonder what was truly in her heart?"

Estate planning for faithful Catholics should include much more than mere instructions for the legal disposition of worldly possessions. Those matters are only a part of the issues that need to be addressed. Often, the most difficult—and for many the most important—questions pertain to issues regarding our Catholic faith. These matters become especially significant when not all members of the extended family are actively involved in the Catholic Church.

How many people truly know that we have a fire for our Catholic faith? More importantly, when we are disabled or dead, will others know how much our Catholic faith meant to us and follow our Catholic wishes? What would it mean to our loved ones if they could use us as a role model for their Catholic faith?

Catholic Faith Declaration™ Questions

The first step when going through the process of Catholic Estate Planning is to answer the following questions to articulate your Catholic Faith Declaration™ so your family has it as a reference before you are disabled or deceased. Providing for your relatives and family members means more than leaving money and property; it can also include leaving a personal legacy. (Note also that when we use the term "disability," we are referring to the physical and mental condition of being unable to manage one's own affairs.)

Catholic Disability Preferences

It is my desire to actively participate in my Catholic faith in the following ways: (Please check the boxes you wish to have included in your Catholic Faith Declaration)

❑ It is my desire for my family to provide for the presence and involvement in my care of a priest, deacon, or pastoral care minister from my parish on a regular basis, and provide access to me at all times.

❑ I wish for my family to assist me in attending Mass in the following way(s):
    ❑ Sunday Mass
    ❑ Holy Day of Obligation Mass
    ❑ Daily Mass

❑ I may not be able to attend Mass; however I would like to receive Holy Communion the following way(s).
    ❑ Daily

❑ Weekly on Sundays
❑ Holy Days of Obligation

❑ I would like to give a Mass stipend:
    ❑ Frequency _____
    ❑ Dollar Amount per Mass _____
    ❑ Parish _____
    ❑ Any needy parish of the Diocese of
    _____

❑ Any Specific Religious Order or Mission
_____

❑ Diocese of _____

❑ If I am unable to do so on my own, I would like someone to pray the Rosary with me:
    ❑ Frequency _____

❑ I would like to celebrate Reconciliation/Confession:
    ❑ Frequency _____
    ❑ I would like Examination of Conscience prior to Confession.

❑ I would like to receive weekly Pastoral Care from my Parish.

❑ I would like to receive the Sacrament Anointing of the Sick with the Prayers of Dying (formally Last Rites), which may include any or all of the following:
    ❑ <u>Celebration of Viaticum</u>: The celebration of the Eucharist as viaticum, food for the passage through death to eternal life.

Please check one: ❏ Within the Mass or ❏ Outside the Mass (Whenever possible, viaticum should be received within the Mass.)

❏ <u>Commendation of the Dying</u>: A priest, or deacon, assists the dying person in his passage out of this world to the Father, in the recitation of prayers. After death, the priest, or deacon, should lead those present in the prayer after death.

❏ <u>Prayers for the Dead</u>: When a priest or minister is called to attend a person who is already dead. A priest is not to administer the sacraments of penance or anointing, but to pray for the dead person using certain prayers. The dead are effectively helped by the prayers of the living. The priest may conclude these prayers with a simple blessing or with a symbolic gesture, for example, making the sign of the cross on the forehead. A priest or deacon may sprinkle the body with holy water.

❏ <u>Rites for Exceptional Circumstances</u>: The exceptional circumstances for which these rites are provided arise when there is a genuine necessity, for example, when sudden illness or an accident or some other cause has placed one of the faithful in the proximate or immediate danger of death.

❏ I would like to maintain my membership(s) in religious or spiritual organizations.

Name of Organization(s): _____

_____

_____

❏ I wish to maintain my registration at my parish.
Parish Name: _____

❏ I wish to be comfortable and as free from pain as possible.

❏ I wish to have family and friends visit me.

❏ I want to have Catholic books, tapes, music, and other materials provided for me.

❏ I desire scripture be read to me:
    ❏ Frequency _____
    ❏ Duration _____

❏ I want to continue my stewardship of tithing during my illness to the following: (Please indicate amount and frequency.)
Parish _____

Diocese Annual Capital Campaign _____

Other Organizations _____

❏ If there are ever any questions at all concerning my care, it is my desire that my family and faithful friends...
    ❏ Lift up all decisions into the hands of the Holy Spirit in and through the Holy Catholic Church and follow the teachings and writings of the United States Conference of Catholic Bishops to include:
        ❏ Ethical and Religious Directives for Catholic Health Care Services
        ❏ Nutrition and Hydration: Moral and Pastoral Reflections.

❏ Other: _____

_____

Catholic Death Preferences

❏ I want to continue my stewardship of tithing after my death to the following: (Please indicate amount and frequency.)

Parish _____

_____

Diocese Annual Capital Campaign _____

_____

Other Organizations _____

❏ It is my wish to have a Vigil Service held so we can come together with our family and friends in prayer. This can also be a memorial service for those who are choosing cremation.

❏ I would like the following stated in my Declaration:

❏ May Christ's presence at my Vigil and God's mercy give you all the strength you need as you call upon our Father to receive me into his kingdom.

❏ As a Catholic, my funeral rite recalls Christ's victory over death. Please pray to seek strength as you face my death.

❏ I would like the specific reading for my vigil:

_____

❏ I would like my family to decide the reading.

❏ Matthew 18:19-20
❏ John 11:21-27
❏ Luke 20:35-38

❑ I would like the Rosary to be prayed at my vigil.

❑ Eulogy: I would like my family to read my Catholic Faith Declaration.

❑ It is my wish to also have a Funeral Liturgy with a full Mass:
  ❑ Opening Song _____

   _____

  ❑ Reception of the Body in the Church

❑ I want my body blessed with holy water symbolizing the waters of my baptism. (A rite automatically done by the church.)

❑ After the procession into the church, I want a funeral pall placed over my coffin reminding me of the garment I wore at my baptism. (A rite automatically done by the church.)

❑ I request an Easter Candle indicating a sign of Christ's presence. (A rite automatically done by the church.)

❑ Please have the following placed on my coffin:
  ❑ Family Bible
  ❑ Family Cross
  ❑ Other:

❑ First Reading - Old Testament Reading:
  ❑ I would like my family to decide the reading (check one).
    ❑ Job 19:1, 23-27
    ❑ Wisdom 3:1-3
    ❑ Wisdom 4:7-15
    ❑ Lamentations 3:17-26

- ❑ Daniel 12:1-3
- ❑ 2 Maccabees 12:43-46
- ❑ Isaiah 25:6-9

❑ Responsorial Psalm:
  ❑ I would like my family to decide the responsorial (check one).
- ❑ Psalm 23
- ❑ Psalm 25
- ❑ Psalm 27
- ❑ Psalm 42
- ❑ Psalm 43
- ❑ Psalm 63
- ❑ Psalm 103
- ❑ Psalm 116
- ❑ Psalm 122
- ❑ Psalm 130
- ❑ Psalm 143

❑ Second Reading (New Testament):
  ❑ I would like my family to decide the reading (check one).
- ❑ Acts 10:34-43
- ❑ Romans 5:5-11
- ❑ Romans 6:3-9
- ❑ Romans 8:14-23
- ❑ Romans 8:31-35, 37-39
- ❑ Romans 14:7-9, 10-12
- ❑ 1 Corinthians 15:20-28
- ❑ 1 Corinthians 15:51-57
- ❑ 2 Corinthians 4:14-5:1
- ❑ 2 Corinthians 5:1, 6-10
- ❑ Philippians 3:20-21

- ❑ 1 Thessalonians 4:13-16
- ❑ 2 Timothy 2:8-13
- ❑ 1 John 3:1-2
- ❑ 1 John 3:14-16
- ❑ Revelation 14:13
- ❑ Revelation 20:11-21:1
- ❑ Revelation 21:1-5, 6-7

❑ Gospel Reading:
  ❑ I would like my family to decide the reading (check one).

- ❑ Matthew 5:1-12
- ❑ Matthew 11:25-30
- ❑ Matthew 25:1-13
- ❑ Matthew 25:31-46
- ❑ Mark 15:33-39, 16:1-6
- ❑ Luke 7:11-17
- ❑ Luke 12:35-40
- ❑ Luke 23:33, 39-43
- ❑ Luke 23:44-46, 50, 52-53
- ❑ Luke 24:13-35
- ❑ John 5:24-29
- ❑ John 6:37-40
- ❑ John 6:51-59
- ❑ John 11:17-27
- ❑ John 11:21-27
- ❑ John 12 23-28
- ❑ John 14:1-6
- ❑ John 17:24-26
- ❑ John 19:17-18, 25-30

❑ Intercessions
  ❑ Specific: _____
  ❑ Prayers _____
  ❑ Closing Song _____

❑ Rite of Committal at Graveside
  ❑ Scripture Verse
    ❑ I would like my family to decide the scripture verse.
    ❑ John 6:39
    ❑ Philippians 3:20
    ❑ Revelation 1:5-6

❑ Prayer:
  ❑ Lord Jesus, Christ, by your own three days in the tomb, you hallowed the graves of all who believe in you and so made the grave a sign of hope that promises resurrection even as it claims our mortal bodies. Grant that our brother may sleep here in peace until you awaken him to glory, for you are the resurrection and the life. Then he will see you face to face and in your light you will know the splendor of God, for you live and reign forever and ever. Amen.
  ❑ Let my family or the priest use a different prayer of their choice.

❑ Concluding Prayer Blessing:
  ❑ God of holiness and power, accept our prayers on behalf of your servant _____ ; do not count his deeds against him, for his heart he desired to do your will. As his faith united him/her to your people on earth, so may your mercy join him to the angel in heaven. We ask this through Christ our Lord. Amen.

❑ Let my family or the priest use a different prayer of their choice.

❑ Cremation
    ❑ I would like my body (ashes) blessed by Holy Water. (A rite automatically done by the church.)

❑ Scripture at Conclusion of Declaration:
    ❑ Psalm 23:

The LORD is my shepherd;
there is nothing I lack.
In green pastures you let me graze;
to safe waters you lead me;
you restore my strength.
You guide me along the right path
for the sake of your name.
Even when I walk through a dark valley,
I fear no harm for you are at my side;
your rod and staff give me courage.

You set a table before me
as my enemies watch;
You anoint my head with oil;
my cup overflows.
Only goodness and love will pursue me
all the days of my life;
I will dwell in the house of the LORD
for years to come.

    ❑ Other: _____

_____

An example of my Catholic Faith Declaration™ follows. Note that while these are my wishes, yours will be unique to your desires and will need to coordinate with local/parish customs and practices.

Catholic Faith Declaration™

"Therefore, stay awake, for you know neither the day nor the hour."
(Matthew 25:13)

Purpose of My Declaration

"Therefore, stay awake, for you know neither the day nor the hour."
(Matthew 25:13)

To my loved ones and dear friends in Christ, may the love of God and his eternal mercy be with you all. It is very important to me that I leave a personal Catholic legacy because scripture reminds us all, "And whoever does not provide for relatives and especially family members has denied the faith and is worse than an unbeliever." (1 Timothy 5:8)

It is too often that important decisions are left to be made by our loved ones during disability or death. Having to guess at our intentions and wishes could be a tremendous burden. It is my duty as a Catholic to ensure my loved ones do not have to guess at how I want to be cared for in the event of a disability or in the event of my death. What follows therefore are my instructions for my care during a disability and upon my death. Please know that it is with great reflection and much prayer these decisions were reached. I ask that you honor them as my loved ones and that you turn to the comfort and love of the Holy Spirit and the support of the Holy Roman Catholic Church in this endeavor.

My Disability

It is my desire to actively participate in my Catholic faith in the following ways during my disability. It is my desire to remain active in my Catholic faith for as long as possible. It is my desire as a practicing Roman Catholic that my spiritual care is provided to me. If I am disabled, I would like to have the presence and involvement with my care of a priest, deacon, or pastoral care minister from my parish on a regular basis. I wish to have a pastoral care minister visit and pray with me. I wish to have delivered to me the precious gift of Holy Communion under both species of body and blood.

I wish to attend Mass on Sundays and on Holy Days of Obligation. Should I request the need to attend daily Mass, I ask that arrangements be made for this. If I am unable to attend Mass, it is my desire that arrangements be made for the Holy Eucharist to be available to me.

I wish to be comfortable and as free from pain as possible. I wish to have family and friends visit me. I want to have access to Catholic books, tapes, music, and other materials.

I want to have Scripture read to me on a daily basis and also to be able to pray the Rosary at least weekly.

It is my wish to receive the Sacraments of Anointing of the Sick and Last Rites to include if applicable Commendation of the Dying, Prayers for the Dead, and Rites for Exceptional Circumstances and Viaticum. It is also very important to me to be able to participate in Reconciliation on a weekly basis.

If there is ever any questions at all concerning my care, it is my desire that my family and faithful friends lift up all decisions into the hands of the Holy Spirit in and through the Holy Catholic Church and follow the teachings and writings of the United States Conference of Catholic Bishops to include the Ethical and Religious Directives of the Catholic Health Care Services and Nutrition and Hydration: Moral and Pastoral Reflections.

Tithing has long been my way of life and joyful answer to the

Father's call as a Catholic. I wish to maintain tithing practices I have in place upon the signing of this document. I wish to continue the flow and the frequency of the dollar amount to my parish in which I now joyously attend and also to the Bishop of Phoenix Annual Capital Campaign. I wish to maintain my parish registration and all other memberships in religious and spiritual organizations I belong to.

Upon My Death

Upon my death I wish that the same consideration be taken to fulfill my wishes. Much prayer has gone into the decisions I now request for my funeral service. As in my life as a Catholic, it is also in my death as a Catholic I wish to actively participate. What follows are my instructions regarding my vigil service, funeral liturgy, selected readings, prayers and music. The instructions for my graveside ceremony are also mentioned.

Do not be filled with sorrow as you see to the details of my requests upon my death. I have gone to my Father and joyously do so with peace of mind and spirit that I not only lived to the best of my abilities as a Catholic but did so with equal effort unto my death. I made these plans without fear and without reservation and with great peace. Celebrate!! For I am home. May the peace and love of my Lord and Savior Jesus Christ be with you all. He is ever present, lean on him, and draw from his love and strength as well as mine.

It is my wish to have a Vigil Service so we can come together with our family and friends in prayer. May Christ's presence at my Vigil and God's mercy give you all the strength you need as you call upon our Father to receive me into his kingdom. I want the following at my Vigil:

Reading: 1 Corinthians 5:6-10

Rosary: I want the rosary prayed.

Eulogy: I want my Catholic Legacy Declaration™ read.

As a Catholic, my funeral rite recalls Christ's victory over death. Please pray to seek strength as you face my death. It is my wish to also have a Funeral Liturgy with a full Mass.

Reception of the Body in the Church: I want my body blessed with holy water symbolizing the waters of my baptism. After the procession into the church, I want a funeral pall placed over my coffin reminding me of the garment I wore at my baptism. Also, I request an Easter Candle indicating a sign of Christ's presence. Finally, please have the family Bible and our family Cross placed on my coffin.

Liturgy of the Word:
Old Testament: Isaiah 25:6-9
New Testament: 2 Timothy 2:18-13
Responsorial Psalms: Psalm 27
Gospel: Matthew 11:25-30.
Songs: Be Not Afraid, Happy Song
Rite of Committal at Graveside:
Reading: Matthew 25:34
Prayer: Lord Jesus Christ, by your own three days in the tomb, you hallowed the graves of all who believe in you and so made the grave a sign of hope that promises resurrection even as it claims our mortal bodies. Grant that our brother may sleep here in peace until you awaken him to glory, for you are the resurrection and the life. Then he will see you face to face and in your light you will and know the splendor of God, for you live and reign for ever and ever. Amen.

Concluding Prayer: God of holiness and power, accept our prayers on behalf of your servant Bradley; do not count his deeds against him, for in his heart he desired to do your will. As his faith united him to your people on earth, so may your mercy join him to the angel in heaven. We ask this through Christ our Lord. Amen.

(From *The Funeral Rites*, copyright 1990 Catholic Book Publishing Company)

My final wish is to have my Trustee set aside money for Mass stipends for Masses said in my honor. I wish to have 20 Masses said for my soul at $25 per Mass. I prefer to have the Masses said at my parish, but if the burden is too great on my parish, the Masses may be said at any needy parish for the Diocese of Phoenix or Tucson.

Psalm 23:
The LORD is my shepherd;
there is nothing I lack.
In green pastures you let me graze;
to safe waters you lead me;
you restore my strength.
You guide me along the right path
for the sake of your name.
Even when I walk through a dark valley,
I fear no harm for you are at my side;
your rod and staff give me courage.

You set a table before me
as my enemies watch;
You anoint my head with oil;
my cup overflows.
Only goodness and love will pursue me
all the days of my life;
I will dwell in the house of the LORD
for years to come.

Dated this _____

_____

Signature

Again, please remember that your parish may have set practices for you to incorporate in your declaration. You may wish to check with a funeral coordinator for information.

Our Wealth

In addition to completing a Catholic Faith Declaration™, as good stewards, we are called to plan for our material wealth. We have discussed the importance of stewardship and giving of our time, talent and treasure. We must also ensure our stewardship continues after we pass away. "Repay to Caesar what belongs to Caesar and to God what belongs to God." (Mark 12:17) Caesar is Internal Revenue Service and State Departments of Revenue.

Building Catholic Bridges

Pontiff refers to our pope and comes from the Latin word pontifex, which literally means bridge builder. Just as our Pontiff builds the bridge between God and humanity, we build catholic bridges between our wealth and our loves or our favorite charity after our death.

The Bridge Builder
by Will Allen Dromgoole

An old man going a lone highway
Came at the evening cold and gray,
To a chasm, vast and wide and steep,
With waters rolling cold and deep.
The old man crossed in the twilight dim,
That sullen stream had no fears for him;
But he turned when safe on the other side,
And built a bridge to span the tide.

"Old man," said a fellow pilgrim near,
"You are wasting your strength with building here.
Your journey will end with the ending day,
You never again will pass this way.
You've crossed the chasm, deep and wide,
Why build you this bridge at eventide?"

The builder lifted his old gray head.
"Good friend, in the path I have come," he said,
"There followeth after me today
A youth whose feet must pass this way.
This chasm that has been naught to me
To that fair-haired youth may a pitfall be.
He, too, must cross in the twilight dim—
Good friend, I am building the bridge for him."

We are all bridge builders. Daily, in both small and great ways, we build bridges of friendship, encouragement, hope, integrity and good will. In the long term, this means that we can build bridges that will benefit those who follow us…or if we build unwittingly, we may build weak bridges that create hardship and despair for those who come after. As Catholics, we have a responsibility to others to build a solid foundation for those who follow: "Tell them to do good, to be rich in good works, to be generous, ready to share, thus accumulating as treasure a good foundation for the future, so as to win the life that is true life." (1 Timothy 6:18-19) Whatever sort of bridge we build, it will likely have a far-reaching effect on the people and things that matter to us most. What kind of bridges are you building?

Income and Estate Taxes

When fulfilling your stewardship calling with Catholic Estate Planning, a basic understanding of our tax system is required. We have come to understand that wealth is much larger than most people think. Our real wealth includes our heritage, our personal and family connections, our ties to our community, and of course, our money and property. Federal Income and Estate Tax law divides our property into two categories: Personal Capital and Community Capital. Personal Capital is that portion of property we can give to anyone we choose. Community Capital, on the other hand, is that portion of our financial resources that must be spent on public purposes, as defined by the IRS.

A portion of our assets will either go to the IRS in the form of taxes—considered a public purpose—or will go into your community in the form of charitable contributions. The difference is in the level of control you have over Community Capital. A taxpayer has zero control over the money that goes to the IRS in the form of taxes. However, a taxpayer can become a bridge builder and have more control over the assets by choosing to use Community Capital for charitable efforts.

Taxpayers can designate the charities that receive their Community Capital, and for what purposes. The donor may direct how soon the charities get the funds, how long the funds will last and who will be involved in administration of the funds. Donors can arrange for members of their family to have a large say in how the money is used. Bridge builders may not have total control, but they will certainly have a lot more control than would exist without planning.

Charitable planned giving is not only about being a nice person. It is about taking charge of the control you can have over your Community Capital to make sure it is used in alignment with the rest of your legacy. It is about making certain the money and property part of your legacy is used in harmony with your heritage, your family connections and your values.

Just how much legacy value is there in paying taxes? Has anyone ever seen a plaque or monument to a taxpayer? What do you feel deeply passionate about? What would you like to create to survive you, to serve as a bridge for those who come after you? Will the bridge you build inspire or discourage others? Will it be a blessing or a burden? What will be the impact of the bridges you are building on the people and things that matter most to you? Bridge builder or taxpayer—it is really your choice.

Charitable Contributions

Catholic charities have a tremendous impact on our society. According to the Catholic Charities USA 2000 Annual Survey, which represents a large percentage of Catholic charities overall, Catholic charitable agencies helped 7,017,845 different people in 2000. The survey reported Catholic charities prepared food or distributed food to 3,929,387 people. These are large numbers and it takes a lot of money to help those in need. The circumstances in our community sometimes make it very difficult to give money to charities. The economy could be in a slump and there may be controversies in our Church. Nonetheless, people still need to be fed. People need clothing and shelter and no matter what our circumstances are, we can usually help others who are less fortunate than we are. Jesus reminds us to help those in need.

Come, you who are blessed by my Father. Inherit the kingdom prepared for you from the foundation of the world. For I was hungry and you gave me food, I was thirsty and you gave me drink, a stranger and you welcomed me, naked and you clothed me, ill and your cared for me, in prison and you visited me. (Matthew 25:34-36)

Choosing a Charity

Many charities serve our Catholic faith and it can be difficult deciding which one is deserving of our time, talent and treasure. Before your donation, research the charity. Get to know the charity. Most charities have a person to contact whose responsibility is to answer your questions. Make sure your Catholic story (Faith and

Legacy Declarations™) aligns with the charity's story. Ensure the charity takes time to hear and listen to your story. After you decide which charity to support, make sure the charity keeps you informed on how your assistance helped the organization.

Gift Annuities

We do not have to be worth millions to take control of Community Capital and keep it out of the hands of the Internal Revenue Service. I shared this Community Capital example with a client of modest means who told me, "I am not going to pay the Internal Revenue Service any more than I have to." She was adamant about her beliefs. After we reviewed her financial resources, we discovered she had some stock which, if sold, would result in a capital gain tax. She decided to transfer the stock to a charitable gift annuity and receive an annuity income payment for the rest of her life. She received an income tax deduction when the stock was transferred to the charitable gift annuity and the charity received the remainder of the annuity after she passed away. The charity was able to use the remaining money to support its mission.

Donor-Advised Funds

Sometimes people do not want to give general gifts to a charity. A general gift is a gift that goes to a charity and the charity can decide how the money is used with no guidance from the person making the gift, like the example above. If someone wants to make recommendations regarding the distributions of a gift, a Donor-Advised Fund could be established.

For example, a married couple is passionate about Catholic education and wants those who cannot afford to send their children to Catholic elementary schools to have an opportunity to do so. The couple can transfer a small amount of cash, securities or other assets to the Donor-Advised Fund that is monitored by the charity. The couple advises the charity on investment decisions and also recommends who should receive the scholarships. The Donor-Advised Fund, named after the couple, designated their children the successor advisors to the charity.

Charitable Trusts and Family Foundations

Others may have more sophisticated Community Capital planning. Jack was a successful businessman and was worth a few million dollars. He was surprised he was worth that much, but when he included his house, IRA's and life insurance it added up. His children had moved away and both of them were financially successful in their own right. Jack was about 80 years old. When he realized his net worth, Jack wanted to reduce his estate and income taxes. This was a serious matter to him, because he was about as tight with a penny as anyone you have ever known. Whenever Jack got a bill for professional services, he would drive his little compact economy car up to the office and haggle over nickels and dimes. One heart-to-heart conversation with Jack revealed that he, like just about everybody, wanted not only to reduce his tax burden but also to leave a legacy. With his attorney's assistance, Jack created a Catholic Legacy Declaration™ and identified what was really important to him.

Jack was very passionate about the value of a good education, both to the individual and to the community. He wanted to help maintain a first-rate Catholic education system in his Arizona town. He also wanted to see his parish finish a building it had started. Jack's attorney helped him create a plan to use Jack's Community Capital to do those two things. The attorney took some of the money that would have gone to the IRS, and created an educational foundation to benefit the Catholic school system in his hometown. Jack determined when the school system would get the money, how long it would last and who could be involved in the foundation. Now Jack's money provides grants to upgrade and enrich the teacher training, and to recognize truly superior teaching.

The attorney also created a charitable remainder trust to guarantee Jack's income for the rest of his life, and then to finish the building. After Jack died, the Church was able to complete the building. Jack named his children to oversee the construction project and also the education foundation. And you know what else happened? Jack was different after that. His friends believed that the process changed his life in a remarkable way.

Jack fulfilled his stewardship by helping his Church and humankind by ensuring the education system in his small town could improve. What will you do with your Community Capital? As a bridge builder, make sure you have a say in determining where the Community Capital goes.

For every million dollars the government receives, its Community Capital spending breaks down as follows:

Deposit Insurance	$ 10,000
Federal Operations	$ 60,000
Interest on Debt	$150,000
Grants to State Governments	$150,000
National Defense	$180,000
Entitlements (Welfare, Social Security, etc.)	$460,000

Source: Renaissance Inc.

How can your Catholic Estate Plan reflect your stewardship calling? What time, talent and treasure can you return to God that will build a strong Catholic bridge that will survive you? There are many other estate planning opportunities to take control of your Community Capital. After you pray and reflect on your stewardship, you may wish to consult attorneys, accountants and financial advisors who will be able to take your Catholic Legacy Declaration™ and align it with your financial wealth to build your "Catholic bridge" for the future. Describing all estate planning tools and options here would be futile because the options are unique to every family legacy. Recommending a specific approach before understanding your Catholic Legacy Declaration™ is like putting the cart before the horse.

Estate Planning Documents

There are some basic legal tools attorneys use when drafting a Catholic Estate Plan. Every Catholic should at least have a living will, health care power of attorney, anatomical gift form, property power of attorney, and a will or revocable living trust.

Living Will or Health Care Directive

A living will, sometimes referred to as a health care directive, is the legal document that outlines your wishes when you are in a permanent vegetative condition. The attorney should discuss the options with you so your family members can uphold your wishes if and when you are unable to do so. The discussion with your attorney should include your desire with nutrition and hydration, and the burden versus benefit of certain medical treatments. As Catholics, we are fortunate to have access to a lot of reading material regarding the sanctity of life. If your attorney cannot help you with this conversation, the pastoral care or grief and bereavement office at your parish should be able to help you.

Health Care Power of Attorney

The health care power of attorney lists who you want to make medical decisions for you if you are unable to do so because of a temporary or permanent disability. In most states, before you are admitted to a hospital, the hospital staff will ask you if you have a living will and health care power of attorney and have statutory forms for you to complete. However, this is usually not the best time to complete these forms because you are usually concerned with the pressing medical condition and might not be in the proper frame of mind to discuss such issues.

Anatomical Gift

The anatomical gift form designates if you want to be an organ donor or not. If you are an organ donor, you can specify what type of organs you wish to donate after your death and even for what purposes you desire like for transplant purposes only or for medical research.

DocuBank™

As mentioned above, during a medical emergency is usually not the best time to make end of life decisions with your living will or certain medical decisions with your health care power of attorney. Worse yet, searching for your living will or health care power of attorney while rushing off to the hospital can create unnecessary stress. Or, what happens if you are traveling away from home and have a medical emergency? One low-cost solution to this confusion and stress is DocuBank™, a service that stores your health care documents, including your Catholic Faith Declaration™. DocuBank™ issues an Emergency Card that can be kept next to your insurance card and driver's license. When needed, medical personnel simply follow the directions on your Emergency Card and your health care documents and Catholic Faith Declaration™ will be faxed to the hospital, usually within 15 minutes. For more information about DocuBank™, call 1-800-DOCUBANK or visit www.docubank.com.

Power of Attorney

The property power of attorney designates who you want to manage your personal and financial decisions if you are disabled. The property power of attorney is used for any property that has your individual name on it. When you have a revocable living trust, your trust owns most of your property and your trustees control that property.

Will or Living Trust

Along with these ancillary documents, part of your Catholic Estate Plan must include either a will or trust. At your death, a will governs all property that is in your individual name. Since a will takes effect at your death, it will not help you during a disability. A will goes through the probate court to prove its validity. Probates typically are not favorable to most because the process is fully public, takes a long time and is expensive.

The revocable living trust is often the answer to those who want to avoid probate. As long as your assets are transferred into your trust (referred to as "trust funding") the trust will control your property during disability and death. Other ways to avoid probate include small estates affidavits and beneficiary deeds.

Personal Protections

Creditor Protection

We live in a litigious society and when anyone is harmed or injured, the first thoughts are of lawsuits. We have a duty to protect ourselves and our loved ones from creditors after we pass away. "Behold, I am sending you like sheep in the midst of wolves; so be shrewd as serpents and simple as doves. But beware of people, for they will hand you over to courts and scourge you in their synagogues." (Matthew 10:16-17) Leaving your wealth to your loved ones in a trust with specific instructions can protect them from their creditors.

For example, when I pass away, my property passes to my wife, Julie, in trust for her lifetime with whatever is remaining passing to our children and charities. I jokingly tell Julie that she must grieve at least 20 years before she remarries. Let us say, after I pass away, Julie is driving down the street, runs a red light and gets into a car accident that severely injures everyone involved. Since she is responsible, a lawsuit could follow and hold Julie liable for a lot of money. What assets of Julie's are at risk to the lawsuit? Every asset that is in her individual name or in the name of her revocable living trust is at risk. However, the wealth and property I left for her in my trust is not subject to the creditor claims. Establishing a trust for your loved ones allows them protection from lawsuits and other creditors.

Divorce Protection

Creditor lawsuits are always foremost in our minds, but what about our in-laws? Is everyone happy with the spouse his or her children or loved one chooses? Maybe not. If you leave your wealth outright to your married children, they will usually title the property jointly with the other spouse in order to stay happily married. If there is an unfortunate divorce, one-half of the inheritance could go to the in-law. One-half of the inheritance is then not available for your grandchildren, if there are any. This is usually not an acceptable option; so many people choose to place the wealth in a trust for their children's lifetimes, with the remainder passing to grandchildren or a charity.

Remarriage Protection

A couple who has been married for a very long time came to see me about estate planning. I discussed the awkward issue of remarriage protection, meaning when one of them passes away, do they feel comfortable that the survivor can protect their wealth if he or she subsequently married. The husband quickly stated that he fully trusted the decisions his wife would make after he passed away and they did not need such a protection in their revocable living trust. The right answer, right? The wife quickly elbowed the husband and lovingly started the finger pointing. "When he was out making the money, I stayed home and raised the children. I had a more difficult job than he did. If I die first, I do not want our money to pass to some newly found friend he meets at the golf or tennis club."

The couple wanted the surviving spouse to sign a prenuptial agreement if they remarried which states that the new spouse of the survivor does not have any right to the money left by the spouse who passed away. Signing a prenuptial agreement protects the children and grandchildren because there is a better chance that there will be money available when the surviving spouse passes away. Also, it protects the surviving spouse from the new marriage because the spouse would know if it is true love and not based on the money.

Addiction or Spending Protection

Wealth without responsibility can be dangerous. What if you leave a substantial amount of wealth outright to someone who is addicted to drugs or alcohol? The wealth could kill him or her. There are some financial and practical downsides when wealth is left in a lifetime trust. Your Catholic advisors can help you determine what is beneficial for your particular circumstances. You may decide to leave your wealth in a trust that reflects your values and beliefs as well as ensures your loved ones are protected from lawsuits, and possibly from themselves. The same protection can be extended to the loved one who cannot effectively manage their financial affairs.

This discussion is by no means an exhaustive look at Catholic Estate Planning. The important thing to know is that estate planning can preserve and perpetuate your core Catholic beliefs and values. Seek Catholic advisors who are trained to understand the complex legal and financial aspects of your wealth and recommend the appropriate vehicle and tools to fulfill your stewardship calling. "Plans fail when there is no counsel, | but they succeed when counselors are many." (Proverbs 15:22)

Procrastination

"Therefore, stay awake, for you know neither the day nor the hour." (Matthew 25:13) Although no one intentionally wants to leave a financial, spiritual or emotional burden for their loved ones, it often happens. As Catholics, our duty is to ensure that our loved ones do not have to play a guessing game. Not planning for our deaths can be a challenge to our loved one because of the burdens we place on them. Many know they need Catholic Estate Planning, but never find the time or feel they have enough time to accomplish it. There are many challenges in our lives and we overcome them with the assistance of Jesus in our heart. Catholic Estate Planning can be a difficult challenge for many because it's not easy to discuss and plan for our deaths. It can be hard reaching out to others and proclaiming our Catholic faith to the world. Mother Teresa wrote a beautiful poem about challenges in our lives.

"Do it Anyway"
by Mother Teresa

People are often unreasonable, illogical & self-centered;
Forgive them anyway.
If you are kind, people may accuse you of
selfish, ulterior motives;
Be kind anyway.
If you are successful, you will win some false friends &
some true enemies;

Succeed anyway.
If you are honest and frank, people may cheat you;
Be honest and frank anyway.
What you spend years building, some could destroy overnight;
Build anyway.

If you find serenity & happiness, they may be jealous;
Be happy anyway.
The good you do today, people will often forget tomorrow;
Do good anyway.
Give the world the best you have, and it may never be enough;
Give the world the best you've got anyway.
You see, in the final analysis, it is between you and God;
It was never between you and them anyway.

Catholic Estate Planning is between you and God. You have an awesome responsibility to God to ensure your Catholic faith and beliefs are followed to further His kingdom on earth.

Instead of leaving behind commotion and confusion, advance planning will allow a scenario like this: "I am so glad my parents had their Catholic beliefs incorporated in their estate planning. It was a relief we did not have to guess their wishes. Their advance planning allowed us to just grieve and celebrate their lives. It also made it so much easier to deal with members of the family who did not share our parents' same commitment to their faith. What a blessing it was that our parents took this important step while they were able to do so."

Final Thoughts

All of our gifts and talents come from God. We must give back our gifts and talents to God by answering our call as disciples. As Christ's disciples, we need to serve as stewards of our vocations and stewards of our Church to fulfill the plan God has for each of us. Prayer and reflection can give us guidance to discover our calling.

Take time now to write your Catholic life story—or at least write down your beliefs and values—so your loved ones know you were a disciple of Christ. Now is the time to act on your stewardship calling. Now is the time to proclaim your Catholic Faith and beliefs so your loved ones have a good foundation to continue. Now is the time to start your Catholic Estate Plan. Your Catholic Estate Plan is a mirror that reflects your Catholic beliefs and stewardship calling. It is a legacy for the loved ones we leave behind.

RESOURCES

Called and Gifted for the Third Millennium (Washington, D.C., National Conference of Catholic Bishops, Inc.,1993).

Brother Loughlan Sofiel, ST, Sister Carroll Juliano, SHCJ, and Sister Rosine Hammett, CSC, Ph.D., *Design for Wholeness: Dealing with Anger, Learning to Forgive, Building Self-Estee*m (Notre Dame, Ind., Ave Maria Press, 1990).

Kennon L. Callahan, *Giving and Stewardship in an Effective Church, A Guide for Every Member* (San Francisco, Calif., Jossey-Bass, 1992).

Richard Strozzi Heckler, *In Search of the Warrior Spirit*, (Berkeley, Calif., North Atlantic Books, 1992).

Henri J.M. Nouwen, *Life of the Beloved, Spiritual Living in a Secular World* (New York, N.Y., Crossroad Publishing Company, 1992).

Stewardship, A Disciple's Response (Washington, D.C., National Conference of Catholic Bishops, Inc., 1993).

Ken Blanchard and S. Truett Cathy, *The Generosity Factor™, Discover the Joy of Giving Your Time, Talent, and Treasure* (Grand Rapids Mich., Zondervan, 2002).

Rick Warren, *The Purpose Driven Life, What on Earth am I Here For?* (Grand Rapids Mich., Zondervan, 2002).

John Eldredge, *Wild at Heart, Discovering The Secret of a Man's Soul* (Nashville, Tenn., Thomas Nelson Publishers, 2001).

ABOUT THE AUTHOR

Bradley L. Hahn and his wife, Julie, have a daughter Claire Irene, and a son Andrew James. Brad and Julie are active in ministry at St. Timothy Catholic Community in Mesa, Ariz., where Brad serves on the Pastoral Council. Brad assists a variety of Arizona Catholic charities in their endowment efforts including St. Timothy Catholic Community in Mesa; the Catholic Community Foundation for the Diocese of Phoenix; and Society of St. Vincent de Paul of Phoenix. Brad is also a member of the Knights of Columbus.

Brad is a national teacher on estate planning and stewardship. His law practice is limited to the areas of estate and charitable planning and small business planning. His charitable consulting practice assists charities in charitable endowment planning and stewardship.

He is also the author of *Your Story as a Christmas Gift* for St. Timothy Catholic Community, December 2000; *Leaving a Catholic Legacy* for St. Timothy Catholic Community and the Diocese of Lafayette Louisiana, 2002; *Catholic Bridge Builder or Taxpayer?* for St. Timothy Catholic Community, August 2002; and *Plan for the Unthinkable, Plan Your Legacy of Faith* for the *Catholic Sun*, Feb. 6, 2003.

Brad is a member of the Arizona State Bar; a Fellow of Michigan State University Institute of Stewardship and Philanthropy; and a graduate of the Esperti Peterson Institute.

For more information or assistance on your Catholic Faith and Legacy Declarations™, Catholic Estate Planning or assistance with charitable endowment planning for your organization using the principles espoused in this book, please contact Brad at 480-627-2444.